25 Main Street
Newtown, CT 06470

Cool

REFASHIONED JEANS

FUN & EASY FASHION PROJECTS

ALEX KUSKOWSKI

Checkerboard
Library

An Imprint of Abdo Publishing
abdopublishing.com

abdopublishing.com

Published by Abdo Publishing, a division of ABDO,
PO Box 398166, Minneapolis, Minnesota 55439.
Copyright © 2016 by Abdo Consulting Group, Inc.
International copyrights reserved in all countries. No
part of this book may be reproduced in any form without
written permission from the publisher. Checkerboard
Library™ is a trademark and logo of Abdo Publishing.

Printed in the United States of America,
North Mankato, Minnesota

062015
092015

Content Developer: Nancy Tuminelly
Design and Production: Jen Schoeller, Mighty Media, Inc.
Series Editor: Liz Salzmann
Photo Credits: Jen Schoeller, Shutterstock

The following manufacturers/names appearing in this
book are trademarks: Rit® Liquid Dye, Sharpie®, Tulip®,
Elmer's®, Craft Smart®

Library of Congress
Cataloging-in-Publication Data

Kuskowski, Alex, author.
Cool refashioned jeans : fun & easy fashion projects /
Alex Kuskowski.
    pages cm. -- (Cool refashion)

Includes index.
ISBN 978-1-62403-701-6

1. Jeans (Clothing)--Juvenile literature. 2. Denim--
Juvenile literature. 3. Clothing and dress--Juvenile
literature. 4. Handicraft--Juvenile literature. I. Title.

TT605.K87 2016
646.4--dc23

                                2014045319

To Adult Helpers

This is your chance to assist
a new crafter! As children
learn to craft, they develop
new skills, gain confidence,
and make cool things. These
activities are designed to help
children learn how to make
their own craft projects. They
may need more assistance for
some activities than others.
Be there to offer guidance
when they need it. Encourage
them to do as much as
they can on their own. Be
a cheerleader for their
creativity.

Before getting started,
remember to lay down ground
rules for using tools and
supplies and for cleaning up.
There should always be adult
supervision when using
a sharp tool.

Table *of* Contents

RESTART YOUR WARDROBE

Ripped **UP** Refashioning

Get started refashioning! Refashioning is all about reusing things you already have. You can turn them into new things that you'll love.

Don't toss your favorite jeans when they wear out. They are a ton of fun to refashion. Use jeans to make headbands, snack bags, or decorative flowers.

Permission & Safety

- Always get **permission** before making crafts at home.

- Ask whether you can use the tools and materials needed.

- Ask for help if you need it.

- Be careful with sharp and hot objects such as knives and irons.

Be Prepared

- Read the entire activity before you begin.

- Make sure you have everything you need to do the project.

- Follow directions carefully.

- Clean up after you are finished.

Basic terms and step-by-step instructions will make redoing your closet a breeze. These projects will help you turn jeans into one-of-a-kind fashion pieces.

DISCOVERING DENIM

Denim is a fun fabric to work with. It's tough and **durable**. It can be used to make almost anything. You can use denim for bags, jewelry, clothing, and more!

WORKING WITH DENIM

IF POSSIBLE, USE FABRIC SCISSORS. THEY ARE MADE FOR CUTTING FABRIC.

WASH ALL DENIM BEFORE USING IN CRAFT PROJECTS.

DRAW WHERE YOU WILL CUT WITH CHALK FIRST TO AVOID MAKING MISTAKES.

Refashion Ideas for Jeans

SUPER SCISSORS

- Cut off the pant legs at the knee to turn them into shorts.

- Turn skinny jeans into bell-bottoms. Cut open the bottom hem a few inches. Sew in extra fabric.

CRAZY COLOR

- Dye or bleach jeans to give them a new **hue**.

- Draw on jeans with a permanent marker.

- Add colorful patches to make jeans pop.

ADD SPARKLE

- Glue gems onto jeans with fabric glue.

- Sew beads onto jeans.

RIBBON RUN

- Add zippers or safety pins to jeans for a punk rock look.

- Glue lace or ribbon on old jeans for a pretty twist.

TOOLS & MATERIALS

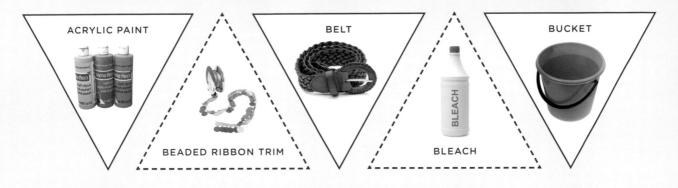

ACRYLIC PAINT

BEADED RIBBON TRIM

BELT

BLEACH

BUCKET

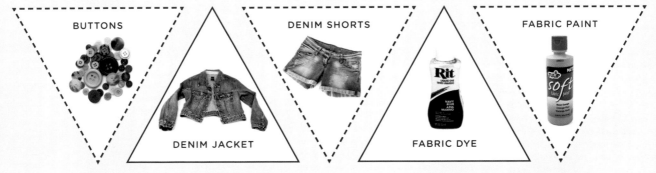

BUTTONS

DENIM JACKET

DENIM SHORTS

FABRIC DYE

FABRIC PAINT

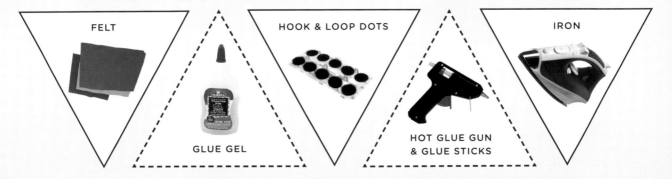

FELT

GLUE GEL

HOOK & LOOP DOTS

HOT GLUE GUN & GLUE STICKS

IRON

HERE ARE SOME OF THE THINGS YOU'LL NEED FOR THE PROJECTS IN THIS BOOK.

IRON-ON FUSING WEB

JEANS

MARDI GRAS NECKLACES

MEASURING CUPS

METAL SPOON

NEEDLE

PIN BACK

PLASTIC BOTTLE

RIBBON

RUBBER GLOVES

SCISSORS

SHARPIE

STRING

THREAD

WHITE JEANS

BLEACH-DYED JACKET

Make a Tinted, Unique Jacket!

1 Fill the bucket with cold water. Get the jacket completely wet. Take the jacket out and squeeze out the extra water. Dump the water out of the bucket.

2 **Crumple** the sleeves of the jacket. Put rubber bands around the folds to hold them in place.

3 Crumple the rest of the jacket. Add more rubber bands to hold the jacket together.

4 Put on rubber gloves. Fill the bucket with 7 cups of cold water and 7 cups of bleach.

5 Put the jacket in the bucket. **Soak** it for 15 to 20 minutes or until it turns white. Turn the jacket in the liquid every 5 minutes. Take the jacket out and rinse it in cold water.

6 Take the rubber bands off the jacket. Rinse it again. Hang the jacket up to dry. Wash the jacket before wearing it. Wash it alone so you don't get bleach on other clothing.

11

WINDING CIRCLES NECKLACE

Get People Seeing Circles!

WHAT YOU NEED

DENIM

RULER

SCISSORS

HOT GLUE GUN &
GLUE STICKS

FELT

RIBBON

1. Cut seven strips of denim. Make them ½ inch by 12 inches (1 by 30 cm).

2. Roll up a strip very tightly. As you roll, add a drop of glue about every 2 inches (5 cm). Put a dot of glue at the end of the strip. Press it down and let the glue dry.

3. Repeat step 2 with the other strips.

4. Arrange the denim rolls on top of the felt. The rolls should touch each other. Glue the rolls in place. Cut the felt around the rolls.

5. Cut two strips of ribbon 16 inches (40 cm) long. Glue one end of each ribbon to the felt. Let the glue dry.

BEADED
DENIM BELT

Buckle Up with a Beaded Belt!

WHAT YOU NEED

JEANS

SCISSORS

RULER

BEADED RIBBON TRIM

HOT GLUE GUN & GLUE STICKS

MARDI GRAS NECKLACE

STRING

THICK NEEDLE

1 Cut off the waistband of the jeans. Lay it on a flat surface.

2 Cut a piece of ribbon trim to the same length as the waistband. Lay the ribbon trim along the waistband. The beads should hang below the bottom edge. Glue the ribbon in place. Let it dry.

3 Cut the Mardi Gras necklace to make a long string. Cut it to the same length as the waistband. Lay it on the waistband above the ribbon.

4 Thread the needle. Push the needle through the waistband from back to front near the necklace. Move the needle to the other side of the necklace. Push the needle through the waistband from front to back.

5 Turn the waistband over. Tie the ends of the string together. Trim the ends.

6 Repeat steps 4 and 5 every 2 inches (5 cm) along the necklace.

15

PAINTED JEAN BANGLES

Make Some Funky Bracelets!

1 Cut a 2-inch (5 cm) section out of the flat part of the plastic bottle.

2 Cut a 2-inch (5 cm) strip out of the jeans. Cut it up the leg of the jeans for a long strip.

3 Glue one end of the denim strip to the inside of the plastic ring. Wrap the denim strip around the ring. Keep wrapping until the plastic is covered.

4 Glue the end of the denim strip to the inside of the ring. Let the glue dry.

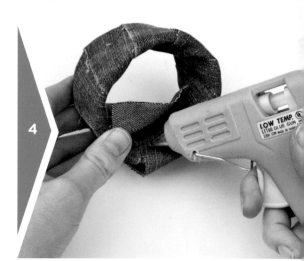

5 Paint a fun **design** on the outside of the bracelet. Let it dry.

Even Cooler!

Use glitter fabric paint for some extra sparkle!

SWEeT
FLOWER PIN

Get Your Flower Power On!

WHAT YOU NEED

JEANS

SCISSORS

HOT GLUE GUN & GLUE STICKS

BUTTON

PIN BACK

1 Cut five circles out of the jeans. Make them all the same size.

2 Fold one of the circles in half. Put glue on one half of the circle. Fold the circle in half again with the glue inside the fold. Press firmly.

3 Repeat step 2 with three more circles.

4 Lay the remaining denim circle flat. Arrange the four folded circles on top of it. The points should face in. Glue them in place.

5 Glue the button to the center of the flower. Glue the pin back to the back of the flower. Let the glue dry.

19

HIP BELT
Pack
Carry Your Phone the Cute Way!

WHAT YOU NEED

JEANS

SCISSORS

IRON-ON FUSING WEB

FELT

IRON

HOT GLUE GUN & GLUE STICKS

HOOK & LOOP DOT

BELT

1. Cut a back pocket off of the jeans. Cut off two belt loops.

2. Lay the pocket face down. Put fusing web along the sides and bottom of the pocket. Place the felt over the tape. Smooth it out. Iron it in place following the instructions on the package.

3. Trim the felt along the sides and bottom of the pocket. Leave 2 inches (5 cm) of felt at the top of the pocket. Cut the corners off the felt at the top of the pocket.

4. Turn the pocket over. Lay a belt loop on each side of the pocket. Make sure they are directly across from each other. Glue the ends of the belt loops in place. Let the glue dry.

5. Press the two sides of the hook & loop dot together. Peel the backing off one side. Press the dot to the front of the pocket near the top. Peel the backing off the other side. Fold the flap onto the dot. Press firmly.

6. Thread the belt through the loops.

21

SPOTTED
DENIM SHORTS

Wear Shorts that Put You in the Spotlight!

1. Lay the shorts out flat. Use a ruler to make a row of dots. Space the dots about 2 inches (5 cm) apart. Make more rows of dots until the shorts are covered.

2. Turn the shorts over and cover the back with rows of dots.

3. Turn the shorts back over. Dip the eraser of a pencil in fabric paint. Use it to cover the dots on the shorts with fabric paint. Let the paint dry.

4. Cover the dots on the back with fabric paint. Let the paint dry.

Even Cooler!

Use several colors of fabric paint to add more color!

DENIM SNACK BAG

WHAT YOU NEED

BELT
RULER
SCISSORS
JEANS
NEEDLE
THREAD

Even Your Food Deserves Some Fashion!

24

Cut the belt 4 inches (10 cm) from the buckle. Then cut the belt 15 inches (38 cm) from the other end. **Discard** the middle part of the belt.

 Cut a pant leg off the jeans just below the knee. Cut off the hem of the pant leg.

3 Turn the pant leg inside out. Put the buckle end of the belt into one end of the pant leg. Line the end of the belt up with the edge of the pant leg.

4 Thread the needle. Tie a knot in one end of the thread. Sew the end of the pant leg closed. Sew the belt end into the seam. Turn the pant leg right side out. Lay it down with the top of the buckle facing up.

5 Sew the other end of the belt to the pant leg about 4 inches (10 cm) from the closed end of the bag. Be sure not to sew through both layers of fabric.

Tattooed
JEANS

Give Your Jeans an Update!

WHAT YOU NEED

WHITE JEANS
SHARPIE
GLUE GEL
RUBBER GLOVES
MEASURING CUP
TABLESPOON
LARGE METAL SPOON
BLUE DYE
SALT
BUCKET

1. Draw **designs** on the front of the jeans with a Sharpie.

2. Draw designs on the back of the jeans.

3. Draw designs near the bottom of the jeans.

CONTINUED ON NEXT PAGE

Even Cooler!

*Use a different color dye for some **trendsetting** jeans!*

1

2

3

27

4 Fill in parts of your **designs** with glue gel. Let the glue dry for at least 5 hours.

5 Put on rubber gloves. Put ½ cup dye, 6 tablespoons salt, and 6 cups hot water in the bucket. Stir it with the spoon.

6 Put the bottom fourth of the jeans in the dye. **Soak** it for 10 minutes.

7 Put the bottom half of the jeans in the dye for 8 minutes.

8 Put three-quarters of the jeans in the dye for 5 minutes.

9 Add 2 more cups of water to the bucket.

10 Put all of the jeans in the dye for 5 minutes.

11 Remove the jeans from the dye. Wring out any extra dye. Rinse the jeans under cold water. Hold them by the waistband so the dye runs down toward the legs.

12 Rinse the jeans in warm water until the water becomes clear. Let them dry.

13 Machine wash alone to rinse out remaining dye and glue.

CONCLUSION

Congratulations! You just refashioned some old jeans. But don't stop here! Take what you've learned to the next step. Try out your own ideas for reusing jeans. Make something **unique** and totally you!

Check out the other books in this series. Learn how to refashion T-shirts, **scarves**, sweaters, and more.

Get crafting today!

GLOSSARY

CRUMPLE – to press something into a ball to make it folded and wrinkled.

DESIGN – a decorative pattern or arrangement.

DISCARD – to throw away.

DURABLE – long lasting and able to withstand wear.

HUE – a color or a shade of a color.

PERMISSION – when a person in charge says it's okay to do something.

SCARF – a long piece of cloth worn around the neck for decoration or to keep warm.

SOAK – to leave something in a liquid for a while.

TRENDSETTING – starting a new fashion or look.

UNIQUE – different, unusual, or special.

Websites

To learn more about Cool Refashion, visit **booklinks.abdopublishing.com**. These links are routinely monitored and updated to provide the most current information available.

iNDeX